Praise for *Laala Kash*

"I happened upon Laala's poems quite by ac
love. Laala has an affinity with words, not ur
an inherent sense of beauty and timing coupleu wiui wisuoiii ueyoiiu iiei yeais
that serves not only to mold incredible word sculptures but also the very
thoughts of her readers," L. Stephen Meck; Editor

"My biggest problem with Laala's work is when I read it, I'm blown away to
such a degree that my feedback becomes inane and the only word that comes
out is 'wow'," Ashley French; Student

"There is a definite candor in Laala's poetry, but a wonderful gift as well for her
readers. Her words are full of insight, compassion, and honesty. A beautiful
collection," Lisa Zaran; author of 5 collections including *The Blondes Lay Content*

"Laala has the ability to take common emotions and shape them in a way that
is both honest and original. Her works are incredibly passionate and very real
and altogether unparalleled," Kyle Lanter; Student

"Rarely does an editor have the privilege of reading a work of such beauty and
passion. Laala captures the human heart and experience in every word of her
astonishingly moving collection," Karen S. Davis; Editor, Author/Photographer
(*Santa Anita Morning Rhapsody*)

"Laala's poetry is not done justice even in this lovely volume. It belongs on the
ink-stained pages of notebooks, scrawled illegally on café napkins and written
in the dark on the backs of forearms. Reading her book is like finding hidden
beauty and to be able to find so much of it, collected altogether? It seems
implausible … Her book makes it possible for me to carry around the kind of
beauty I'd otherwise to be looking for," Zoë Migicovsky; Student

"Laala's words are like a warm fresh breeze on a walk among forgotten moments
in the readers' life," Julie Miller

"When I first came across Laala's work, I knew I had found someone worth
reading. Her simple expressions and soft emotions make her easy and refreshing
to read," Preston Adams; Electrical Engineer

"When I read Laala's words, I feel as if I've been lifted out of my world, my
reality, and brought to the window to witness hers. I feel as if she allows me to
come through the window and, when that happens, my life is touched and
forever changed," Trish Wilson

"Often I find myself bleeding inside from Laala's words, for they are daggers that
penetrate deep within my core … In the end, the sheer power of her
magnificently woven tales, poetry, and prose leaves me purified," Niki Casanova

Behind the Mask:
A folded

Laala Kashef Alghata

a poetry and prose collection

First published in 2006 by
HCC
P O Box 10865
Manama
Kingdom of Bahrain

L.D. 4940/2006
ISBN 99901-10-24-7

Digital layout by **Ali Marhoon**

Printed and bound in Kingdom of Bahrain by
Dar Akhbar Al-Khaleej Printing Press

"We can make our own cards by folding our hearts in half and maybe someday giving them to that special one who looks at us through a rain-speckled window and smiles."

So, Laala Kashef Alghata

I.

Ink Bleeds

Matters of the heart

Painted Hearts

We walk around with hearts painted
onto our hands in blue; dead, cold
hearts like all we're surrounded by,
with our hands on our hearts like
a promise, an oath—a salute from
one broken-hearted girl to another,
linking hands to create connections.

Sparks of love, friendship, alluring lies,
attracting all of us who want hearts
in our hands, not painted but beating,
a deep, clotted maroon; breathing, alive.

Hearts Thrown in Shadows

I wonder when our unspoken needs will be forever
fulfilled better than our spoken wishes are, when
we find someone who paints our hearts' emotions
in the sky everyday because he says, "The sky is dull
as it is, just blue. You make it come alive everyday
and in every way. You breathe, you make me
come alive under your touch." And your lips meet
under the covers of illusion and compassion, grip
onto this chimera of love and forever, while you promise
never to say never (what a paradox we all are). For
who really knows what life is about to bring around
the corner of our lives? The one we passed by everyday
without looking closely into the shadows and realising
that our hearts were thrown aside amongst the dust
gathering on the sixty-ninth street across from house
one-oh-one. Breathing in dust and choking as you realise
why you felt so dead when you were alive, you wipe off
the dust and take your first breath of freedom
from that darkness that consumed you.

My Heart: Bruised

My heart: bruised;
some parts: absent;
the beats: uneven;
the pulse: irregular;
the feel: ablaze;
the result: choking;
the endgame: crying.

Open Welts

Doubled up in pain, I wonder what transpired to turn me into a sniveling child—does my memory serve me or another? Wonder if this acuteness is the hurt spoken of when someone you love opts and resolves to attack you (why, why, why?).

.

Not a physical attack, I assure you—no, never that. I can hold my own then. Not an attack with arms or legs; my high kick would break his nose. No, my dear. An attack with all the prose you exposed to him, highlighting your weaknesses. The weaknesses that none knew of—how could they know, when you laugh so loud?—but are now only apparent because you chose to let them show (but not parade them, never parade).

I showed him the pink tissue on my skin (the contrast it made), the scars that healed over time but were still more sensitive than any other part of me. I showed him open welts—the bandages are no help—with droplets of scarlet oozing out, landing on sheets so grimy; and these are regularly cleaned. I showed him my utter despair, how I thought I would never leave this cage, this absolute confinement. I showed him how I banged at the bars and tried to squeeze through, the ridges on my pride as a result—what can hurt a person more? Lastly, I subtly showed him my longing for love, simply to be held, wanting warmth.

Someone clarify to me how he did not comprehend; is stupidity or ignorance the answer? Elucidate, if you please, why any given person would think it amusing and humorous to pick another's scabs, and laugh throughout doing so (a chortle or a snigger, I shall never know).

As I sit and mourn fresh crimson tears and new-fangled incisions (as if I do not have enough), I try to turn my thoughts from them. But alas I cannot. And once again I return to the land of speculation, where nothing is definite. Tell me, what would he do if he saw stained sheets that sang of my woe? If he happened to come across a piece of my skin, peeled off as a memoir (would he cry or dance with joy?). Enlighten me with the knowledge of whether or not his empathy extends to my pain and suffering. Report on, when he is not with me, what truth emits from his mouth?

As my eyes cry their last tears and my cut releases its last drop, I collapse (out of this world). And in the midst of my mentality, I find courage in this new world, these new colours. My heart begins to beat again, and I journey through my mind,

deserted,

beaten,

and alone.

Distant Heartbeats

I read words and smile
tears flooding over
the rims of my eyes
and soft soot eyelashes
wiping their residue
on cheeks so warm
yet cold to touch.

I feel diamonds travel
down past hollows
in the painting
of my face, my life,
and settle on faded lips.

My brown eyes, bruised
with things they have seen
in this world,
this short life of existence.

Fingers press keys
gazing at a screen,
wondering–
when will we meet again?

Distance is one thing
I fear, like every mile
has taken away a smile
that could have been.

Distance means
my fingers pressing
melodies with keys
instead of into your arms
as I pull you into my embrace.

Distance is
a form
of torture.

Distance can
be overcome.

And I do,
but I hate these miles,
as each is a rung in a
    L
    A
    D
    D
    E
    R
that lasts
near-ever.

I miss you
& you have
no idea how much
I whisper
that into the silence.

When will we next
be together?

Diamonds
travel down.
Again.
Again.
And
again.

(Please keep
a hold of my heart.)

Each mile takes away
a smile that could've been
but with your fingerprints
on my heart, each mile
brings us a heartbeat
closer, closer, closer.

Dispirited Love

Your arms are strangers,
a pair of twigs extended
that grasp but don't hold,
and my heart slithers
to the floor and is stepped on,
breaking the fragile veins
pulsating with love
unconditional, through
dying roses and strained smiles,
how fingers grasp fake pearls
through phony kisses
like they're a defeated rosary.

I used to be a shell, once hollow;
now, I'm filled with dispirited love.

Valentine's

This is a day to exchange hearts
dripping with fountains of your love
embroidered with roses and smiles,
filled to the brim with adoration
and devotion.

This is a day of holding hands
and tight hugs, warm bodies
instead of cold and lonely,
a day of standing together
in a heart shape showing
the world our affection.

This is a day for kisses (even
the chocolate kind) and candy,
saccharine at the roof of your mouth,
a day of indulging your sweet tooth
and small cups of espresso
to soften down sugary smiles.

This is a day of being together,
gripping hearts and pressing
fingers together in a blood oath
of forever, a day of dance
and happiness like wind chimes
in a strong breeze, like dreamcatchers
circling overhead.

This is a day of love.
Today is not that day.

Immortal

Vine leaves wrapped around
my arms like your fingers
around my heart, which drum
a soft, steady beat, interrupted
by several loud bangs that move me
to dance with you in your arms,
stepping on your feet in rhythm,
and I close my eyes because my life
is a poem and you're in every line,
creating beauty, giving rhyme.

When Love was Innocent

I remember when love was innocent,
something yelled at the top of our lungs
wondering who could say it louder
(I LOVE YOU!) between each square
of hopscotch as we balanced ourselves
and our lives, connecting with each other
and skipping together (inside, outside,
inside, scales), passing slices of pizza
along to the next person and knowing
how wonderful sharing was, sitting
in groups of ten, fifteen, and never
feeling left out or insecure, you just belong.

I remember when love was innocent
and we used a crayon to draw a heart
on the asphalt in the playground, writing
down all our names inside and smiling.

Child Naïveté

He took her hand and led her to the stream, where the fish glittered underneath the surface like plastic eyes. A small wave crashed gently onto the shore, foaming at their unclad feet as the immense sheet of blue sparkled.

"Now I know that we're just a drop in the sea," she remarked, kicking a pebble with the side of her foot. "I never believed it before. I always thought we were the sea."

"You can be anything you want to be," he replied.

"Not anything."

"Close enough. Come here and look." He pushed her further in.

"Look at what?"

"At how the sea has borrowed the rainbow's colours. See, there's a colour for every part of the rainbow."

She looked and saw the different hues weaving themselves into the water, but never blending. "Yes, I see. The fish think they're more beautiful than the rainbow; or maybe the rainbow decided that the fish needed its colours more than it did."

He smiled and nodded. "There are always some fish in the sea, but not always the ones you want."

"But today they're all there," she smiled, "and I think, just maybe, today is perfect."

Butterfly Smile

I don't know what I'm looking for
when I look into your eyes, but I know
that I want to see you smile.

I imagine the corners of your mouth
like wings on a butterfly, fluttering
against my frown and making me
smile against your touch, fleeting and wonderful.

Much Ado (About Nothing)

I thought that you were my Benedick
and I, your Beatrice, that we argued
against love into love, but oh! I was wrong.

Beatrice truly loved Benedick,
and he loved her. Their fights
were a vibrant cloak to veil their emotions.

No, darling, you were my Claudio,
and I, your Hero, for their love
was of the superficial kind.

Fair Hero, you only loved what your eyes
saw before you, you only loved
who you thought a great man.

Foolish Claudio! How you jump to conclusions
of the maiden you are to marry, how you break
her heart and cast her aside.

(And you killed her once but she came back
to life; no thanks to you and your selfish ways.)

Love is too tricky a treat to play with;
we are, none of us, fit to add to the ingredients
but are, all of us, allowed to stir.

Yes

Yes. Yes. Yes.

I rub my hands together in practiced glee. I have finally found my source. My wisdom, my truth, my naïveté, my lies, my dreams. What shall I do with it now? What should I do with it now? I don't know.

Can you play with wisdom? Can you mix it with a paintbrush and brush it across the sky, painting roses and lilies in the clouds? Can I? Teach me how to show the world what I've learned; I can paint a fracture of the emotion in heartbreak, but I can't paint it in the sky. I've only got this white slip of paper waiting to be filled. Where's my sketchbook? Where's that big A1 field?

I found the truth of my lies. I found out why glittering obscenities slip past my rosebud lips so easily. My love, I will always think of you. It does not matter that I do not love you anymore. You rest so easily on my mind. Your phantom touch brings a smile to my weary face. I try to brush my tears away and the glass shows me streaks of black down my rouge-covered cheeks. I look every inch the fallen angel.

I can't play with my wisdom. It's above that. But my naïveté likes to tease me often, and I seem to play along. All dressed up; a vision in brown velvet, hair shining under the starlight. Don't look past the paint, my dear, don't try to look inside. Peel off this short velvet dress. Take off these tight brown boots. Slip me into my haven and kiss me goodnight.

A trigger
that goes off
by itself.

That's what my lies are like. I don't mean to. I don't. I don't. But I have to lie. I have to keep myself safe, you safe, everyone safe. I have to protect you all and keep everyone from this cocoon I've strapped myself into. I love you. I love you.

How do you know when it is that I lie?

Kiss me goodnight and send me smiling to my [reality]. I tilt my head back and laugh as I course through the streets, watching the motion pictures flickety-flick and smoke rising from abandoned cigarettes. Make me stop abandoning my beliefs in my sleep and make me quit dreaming in neon. Sleeping beauty, sleeping faerie, sleeping frightened girl. Wake me from this self-induced coma. Bring me back. To [fantasy].

An Equally Wonderful Girl

I've got dreamcatchers hanging above my bed to trap
out the nightmares and deliver what I long for, but
I've always said we have to be our own dreamcatchers
and I think we're that for each other.

You say if words were for people who mean the most
then I'd have many to hang like wind chimes and I would–
just to decorate my room with your beauty and talent
and show the world that there's this wonderful girl
out there who is my soul sister and couldn't be more
wonderful than she already is.

We press our nibs down onto paper to stain the sheets
with our woes and explain to each other the details of
our misery or happiness; like pressed flowers our words
are beautiful as they decay, a hint of an aroma still there.

We plan surprises because it makes us smile to have something
to do for the other and to get something from the other, be it
a poem or a call. We're fortunate enough to realise this
is rare, we've been lucky to have found each other across
these miles and connect so deeply we wonder sometimes:
are we long-lost sisters or just two girls who have been blessed?

Your Flawless Poet

I love you because the folds of your lips cup
so many raw wounds not quite ready to be spilled
into words, but more than ready to be spilled into me,
because you say I'm your writer, that I should write
what you think because no one's been able to
get into your mind better than I, and that you had never
considered writing beautiful until you saw mine and how
I'm apparently flawless as I type. You said you wanted
me, but you got my words instead—and I'm sorry,
but my words and I are one being you can't ever separate,
because even as I touch you a poem is forming
in my mind of images that turn into words as quickly
as a spider spins its web. But you're beautiful, darling,
so much more beautiful than I, and it's because of you
that I find these words. Let my pen dance alone
when you're around, as you grasp me tightly, telling
me that I should never leave and that you never want to be

alone.

Such a One

You trade my anger for smiles and laughter
and say I'm beautiful and wonderfully clever.
You promise that I will someday smile, looking
ahead without disasters obscure, you would
hold out your pinky and promise me forever, only
because you think I'm worth it. You have stood
by me and watched me waver, gently steering
me back. You ask me to be strong, brave; sound
and safe within my heart, and say you know
how much I'm worth and that I'll never know
how much that is. You call me your favourite
pearl and say, "Before you, the rest fall to the floor."

I don't know how I managed to find such a one,
ingenious and caring, who loves me so, unsure
whether I deserve all the care you have for me,
but I try to live up to what you've made me
and when I don't, you love me still, you call me
the cure for weariness, say I'm responsible for
your surges in power (someone, please tell me
how I managed to find such a one) and vow
that it's only within the constraints of my smile
that you realise, repeatedly, life isn't over yet.

Goodbye, My Dearest

Hold me in your arms tonight
as we smile at each other
and I trust you when you say
"We need to let go," because
I've got my reasons that are
also yours, hold me tight, safe,
and make this night seem like
a forever moment, and the only
words I focus on are "trust me,"
emitting from your lips.

Hold my hand as I begin to cry
and just smile when I say
"I love you"; turn away and whisper
our heartfelt goodbye.

Yours

Like a friend I defend against rumors
that fly with or against the breeze
currently playing with your hair;

Like a lover I stand protective
when someone dips their fingers
into your heart to taste;

Like a soulmate I understand the depth
of the emotions that tinkle your heartstrings
like a badly played violin;

Like a stranger I stand apart to watch
as your life continues within its strand
and you paint lullabies into my pen.

His Forever Age

She doesn't know his last name, because he says it's dead and buried under mountains, its blood running wild with the river, flowing to the sea to be forgotten like he once was. So she asks him his age and whether or not he can love, and he tells her that he first fell in love at seventeen. She asks if that, then, is his age; he replies, *It forever will be*. She says, *Great answer*, and smiles like the wind, wild and free.

History of Us

I make everything sound pretty
on paper, but you slaughter me
daily, you leave behind a massacre,
and maybe I should write a song
to sing to you, maybe I should
nickname you General Giap, because
you always launch an offensive against me.
You kill me. You love to recreate
Dien Bien Phu, as if it's something
to be proud of. And perhaps
I should just let you go. The French
crashed and burnt, but I refuse to.

I won't be written down in history
as just another failure. Prince Paris
is not you, and I'm not Queen Helen;
so let us part, and stop igniting wars
that we can't help put out.

Our love isn't that strong;
it's a spark, not a flame.

Technicolour Abandoned

Like toy soldiers standing alone, we don't need
someone beside us, but we want someone there
to fill the empty space in our hearts and between
our fingers like claws or bitter steel. We will wrap
around each other with promises of eternity before
we decompose into piles of dust and earth, before
we stand amongst the pain and cry out. We bleed
onto paper to immortalize words, drip our hearts
between pages to save the colour of our ache
for the future when technicolour is abandoned
and grayscale adored, when we turn back
into the black and white photographs of
our grandparents, fragile dust settling on porch chairs,
lights dim or brilliant sunshine, contrast within lives,
the sun just a ball of white, colour filtered
from the world, we disappear into our hearts to find
what was once beautiful, seemingly forever lost.

Empty Echo

Freeze me with your lips
and let the light pass through
your fingers, like streaks
of spilled golden honey.

Wrap me in your arms and let us struggle through life together. I beg
you to let me into your heart, but you're not in mine. I want you to be
but my heart's shot to pieces and I don't know how I'm supposed to
put the slivers back together again and feel. I'm devoid of everything,
and God, I hate being a cliché, I hate being a cliché so much; but I am,
I just am. I want to dance under the starlight and have you kiss me, but
I want to learn how to feel before we start our circle of "love." How is
it that I know I care about you but my heart's just an empty echo of a
throb? How is it that I've forgotten how to cry when these tears spill
over my cheeks everyday? Make me remember how to live because
there's more than one way of suicide, and letting myself go feels like
suicide and I don't know how to stop this. I don't know how to return
to being me. "I love you" is sweet but it has lost its meaning. When you
tell me you love my words, tell me what you love about them because
these are just words. I have no actions and I'm not beautiful or smart
or clever. I'm not even me anymore.

Wipe away my tears
of blood, stains leaving
a trail of footsteps no one's
meant to follow.

II.

Beyond the Body

Matters of the mind

City of Limbo

This city is a blur of smoke and peeling billboard ads, of people meeting, greeting, being, leaving—all in one night. This is a town of sometime hellos, forever goodbyes, and perhaps a few hours of freedom in between. We walk alone, stepping on burning cigarettes, fumes swirling to form silky curves in the air, walking to our destination because we're all damned anyway. We turn our heads away from fake smiles and cheap kisses, defeated handshakes and heartless hugs.

(Welcome to Limbo. We're all dead in this city.)

The sidewalks should be framed and mounted as the greatest works of action art, expressionism and graffiti meeting in swirls. The place is rough and unrefined, sand sprinkled in your hair from the crumbling walls, fingers bleeding from careless cuts.

(The city is made of texture and blood. Come visit sometime.)

The sky here is grey mixed with green; we've forgotten what blue looks like. Clouds meet and kiss in mid-air, forming forgotten images of aeroplanes and automobiles. We left technology behind years ago; that's no longer part of our world. We move slowly and carefully, with hot cocoa blistering our lips to beautiful shades of maroon. Our nails are short and filled with crust; we are a part of the earth and the earth a part of us.

(Our city smells of copper and lies.)

Ignore the alleyways and the glittering needles; what you don't see does not exist. We carry our pills in our pocket, pills of different colours popped like sweets. We're dependent on this; we live in this grime because we're made of it. Don't try and scrub anything away; we like our smiles upside down and the bags won't disappear from underneath our eyes. Take in our throbbing veins and understand.

(This city exists inside each of us.)

We're all a little psychotic.

Death

Cracked lips whisper prayers into darkness
with shades of gold dissecting the room
throwing hues around, rays that try
to disappear the shadows in my heart
and soul, corners no one dares to see
(I am dead). Death is barely a period
on a page; it flows seamlessly into another
wor(l)d, another life, leaves behind one soul
and picks up another to see through.

Life is what we cannot put between
two lines of grey, too many colours
to contrast each other so beautifully.
Life cannot be fit in between grey because
even the depressed have different hues
within their eyes and between the strings
of their heart, beating itself (to Death).

Death, "Goodnight"

He's quiet, stares out of windows like the blinds
are made of diamonds and gold, the sunlight
reflected in his peppered hair, silver strings like
magnesium, catching fire and reacting brilliantly
as the light hits them, his head on fire, startling
contrast to his dark skin and almost-black eyes.

He sits reflecting on aged days gone by, times
past, and wonders when his old friend will appear
again, when Death will reappear to kiss him
goodnight, take him gently into the hollow between
the earth and sky, lay him down and close his eyes,
make him relive his life in his grave;

yesterdays past.

Panic

You struck a match under my eyelids
to see the fury of my tears; you watched
me gasp for air as my throat closed up,
as I dug my fingers into my chest,
pushing down against my heart to try
and pump some life back into me.

You waited to see what would happen
as I fell to the ground, light-headed
from lack of air. I've never been that way
before, never had to gasp for air on ground,
though I did nearly drown once or twice
in the middle of the sea as I pushed around
trying to find the shore.

I've had my share of tears, glistening
on my eyelashes and cheeks, reddening
my face in a natural blush, but I've never
cried that hard. How the next morning
despite the eye drops my eyes remain
swollen, the edges a deep red. How I feel
the tears brimming underneath still
prickling, though I am not sobbing anymore.

It scares me how a two-year-old's fist
could knock me over this morning as I slouch
and eat spoonfuls of honey to try and regain
some energy. Legs are almost no support
and I feel my way around, grasping doorframes

and handles as I step on my glasses
and complete the murder of my sight.

One night of your (deserved) anger squeezed the life out
of me; I can't imagine having to live with it all the time.

Afraid

I'm afraid if I speak too loudly
the window panes will shatter
and create a beautiful mosaic
of reflected images, sky blues
and grass greens distorted to produce
beautiful masterpieces worthy of frames
and compliments as Picasso's are.

I'm afraid that if I walk too fast
you won't bother to catch up
and leave to turn and walk away
from me down another path, another
memory lane riddled with happiness
minus me, and leave me stranded.

I'm afraid that when I leave this land
I'll forget that I love it and fall in love
with another, and won't want to move
back, for the soil here is constantly damp
with all of my tears, dirt clinging to me
like a second skin. The memories here
are too many; this terrain has seen me
go through too much pain to be naïve.

I'm afraid when you hug me tomorrow
you'll be hugging me for the last time,
because every time I see you another
part of me dies. Mouth-to-mouth
will not save me, but it hurts that none

have tried. Push down on my chest
and make my blood flow, make my heart
beat again as you move my limbs
into the safety position; but my safety
is only with you, so hug me goodbye.

I'm afraid that when the lights
are out, my demons will visit again,
because they don't seem to like parting me
for too long. Demons taking on shapes
of people I think I know and think I love,
trying to hurt me in my dreams as much
as they hurt me unconsciously in my wake.

I'm afraid of pain; I don't even like to see
others'. They told me once to become
a doctor, help those in need, and I turned
away from them. I would love to contribute
but I can't stand blood, but even more
can't stand to see people in pain. Releasing
that pain would be amazing, but I can't
suffer through the ones I wouldn't save
and watch the ones I would suffer first.

I'm afraid of being afraid, of how nothing
in my life is real anymore, how they tell me
to trust when all I've ever been is let down.

Do They Really Call Her Beautiful?

When will you start to eat? When will I be able to wean you away from all this trash? You poke once-soft skin and frown, tugging at muscles in your jaw to distort your once-upon-a-time gorgeous features. Ivory-coloured bumps are appearing beneath bruised elastic skin, which slowly stretches over bone. *And where are* **you***?* You're lost in an asinine, dangerous world full of "ana loves you, baby" pop-ups. Ana doesn't love you. ANorexiA is a disease, not a lifestyle. I love you—and hate that you're doing this to yourself.

I remember how it used to be between us, dashing around full of energy and wonder. Why did it all have to change? Laughing as we grabbed our sides and each other's hands, tumbling into a pizza place to discover ourselves in a bar. Darling, we were drunk; drunk on the high we got together. *So why did it all have to change?* We grew up, that's why. We each took a trip to hell (and back again), and we haven't sat down and told the tale all in one go. It would take too long, be too emotional, and would probably break one of us. When we stand on my patio, safe from the drizzling rain, do you ever wonder what happened to the old us? *You know, the ones who would've taken one look at rain beginning to glitter up a window and rushed outside to dance and swallow every drop of God's salty tears.*

Remember when we could look at an ice cream van without worrying about the calories? Without one of us counting them and the other knowing the danger surrounding food? Remember how we'd just bet that one of us would get a smudge of dairy across her tank top? When was the last time you sucked on a flake and just laughed when it crumbled in your mouth, falling in chocolaty slivers to the floor? Damn those scales (*flicker, beep, number*)! Just throw them out the window.

You used to say you would always believe me. I promised you I'd never lie. What happened to those promises?

And when you decide Ana isn't for you, that she's not that close a friend, you turn to your other. Mia's a darling, is she not? She offers you sugary close-lipped smiles (*rotting teeth would be a turn-off*) behind long eyelashes and defined cheeks. You don't look inside her, darling, and I don't blame you. Who would want to see a burning gullet? BuliMIA takes you in and you put me out. Is there only space for one in your heart? Tell me: do you love me? Because I can't see you anymore. Because I don't know if you're you. My old friend, my best friend, she loves me, I know. This girl in front of me just tries to hide her two new closest friends from me. She pretends. I wonder how well she will act when I see her brittle bones broken, her body lifeless and cold. Will this disorder be the nail in her coffin? Still she feints.

All our promises thrown out, these lies flourish and begin to take on a certain charm for her. I watch the reality. I sit, watch this pitiful horror movie, and weep.

It's sad seeing you turn and pull away from the ones who love you.
It's even more so seeing what you've turned into.
It's sad not knowing if I'll ever have you back again.

But the saddest thing, sweetheart? Knowing that you were so *much more beautiful* before this all started.

Ash Wires

Your arms are wires and just as thin,
just as bendable, and I worry that
when I hug you you might snap and break
and I'll have to fix the pieces of a girl
I once knew and once loved—tall, but
with slits in her wrists like valleys of crimson,
blood rolling on skin like the waves
roll on the shore, splashing and spilling
over. With that cigarette in your lips
as you preach against smoking,
the end glowing. They say that
in the war, the third one to take a drag
would be the one who would get shot,
because the first would be spotted,
the second aimed, the third gone—
and I wonder, which one are you? Is there
still a chance I could save you, pull
you down, away from harm's way, or
are you taking the third smoke and
seconds away from being obsolete?

You're a fragile piece of art, one that
I would create in class with mud rock
wrapped around supports hanging in air.

How do you stop the fallen from falling?

A Great Divide

A conflict is taking place inside of me and I no longer know which side is winning, or which side I want to win. The two are forced to the negotiating table and how I wish I could be split in half, divided along a parallel like Vietnam was along the seventeenth. Two separate parts would then exist, but does that even solve anything? Because if Vietnam's anything to go by, the fights continue. They persevere, even when the people don't. I'm sick of being general over two armies and I'm sick of having to think in two different ways. Like Dorian Grey, but I've got the portrait in my heart and my appearance doesn't change. I've remained invariable for the past five years. People look at me and smile and ask me when I'm going to age. But my heart withers with their smiles and laughter, it shivers when they put their arms around me and claim to be my friends. I wish it would stay alive, not in a cardiac unit but alone, when it's shot down by love. I'm strong, alright, but that depends on how long I have to be so. Even Castro's days are numbered.

I'll swim to the shore, if you'll only tell me that this is the sea.

Bitter and Oppressed

Disappointment oozing through my veins
like a disease, throbbing behind my eyes
tauntingly, infecting my body and soul,
pinpricks that are tangible, obvious, felt
by the blind, running their thumbs across
my pumping heart, tracing the bumps
and bruises, trying to smooth down rebuffs
and anger. My lips are dry, crackling; hard
to speak or talk, my throat is parched
and scratched, like cats' claws along
my trachea begging to be released.

My voice vibrates within me, but I bite
down and remain silent, mute, expected
to follow all the rules, until the day I break
free, when my exemplar exterior dissolves,
when I'm no longer the one you've always
known you wanted to be.

I'm just no longer.

Potter's Wheel

I'm just a big mound of clay spinning
on your potter's wheel as you beat me
repeatedly to try and shape me, make me
perfect, but I've been left out too long
and instead of slipping between your fingers
and letting you throw me, I'm cracking,
breaking. You have to learn when
it is you've gone too far and the clay
is just too hard to work with, too tough
to change.

You have to learn how to let me be myself.

Texts of Emotion and Unique Fingerprints

My senses are imbedded deep within my mind's monastery
with monks scribbling in focus to copy texts of my emotions
to record feelings and lies into my subconscious and desert
me in my reality, to make me able to wake from dreams
of all-consuming darkness, of my heart disappearing
and dissolving with acid to corrode life, those that I hold precious
unavailable, miles in between some of us and lies between
the others, such tight knots that life knits in the canvas
of our skin, irreplaceable prints of significance making
everyone unique unto themselves, a fingerprint to the world,
but an identity to me.

III.

Footsteps

That which is life

For Zoë Migicovsky

So

So, we do what we do and we try to breathe because they say that if we don't we'll die. But don't they know that we're already dead inside and our little hearts are rotting? But they're not so little, they're big and once upon a dirty world we didn't know how much we could love. We were so deep in ourselves, in what we had to do, and those who passed us by should all know what they missed. But do you know what? Its okay, because who wants Hallmark clichés anyway? We can make our own cards by folding our hearts in half and maybe someday giving them to that special one who looks at us through a rain-speckled window and smiles. And he can be the only one to read all the poetry we've ever written.

So, we cry (with dry eyes) because they say we're cold-hearted if we don't. Then they can't tell when we're really crying (these tear stains are nothing to go by). We can't think and don't want to, really, but we're stuck in this circle going round and round. (Are you dizzy yet? I am.) And who was it who said, "Circles go on forever"? Because we don't have forever, but they treat us like we do. Then they ask us "Whatever happened to being young and carefree?" and we just want to turn around and kick them until they start to bleed because if they really wanted us to be carefree they'd let us go.

So, we want to have time but we have to "make" time and damn if that isn't the most annoying thing to have to say. You said you were less tangible when you were in love, and God I'm still trying to figure out if I agree. See, the last time I was in love (when?) I drifted from being a shadow to being the most colourful butterfly. I was the recluse and the class queen rolled into one. (And when have I not been a paradox?) I know you, darling, you know me, we know each other; because sometimes when I read you I feel like I'm reading myself and I wonder why a part of me is somewhere else in the world. Though I don't know you and I haven't seen you, so when was the last time you were in love? You say you feel lonely and I do, too, but when we look up at the same sky we don't see the same stars.

So, we don't even want to be a part of this world any longer, or at least, want to get out of the one we're in. No, this isn't a suicide wish, but I feel like every letter I send is saying goodbye. Wouldn't it be easier if we only worried about us? For when was the last time we walked out the door and didn't count the minutes we'd be away and how much we didn't want to go back? I'm like a puppet with strings and they keep pulling me back and I struggle and you do, too (like we always do), and do these people still think we're beautiful when we're just a heap on the floor?

So, I don't really know what I'm saying but I try to make my words worthy of Eid, but the money I see is crisp and clean and my words are just words that have been regurgitated. (And they say I'm unique.) Yeah, we don't know what we're saying but we know that we like to string these words together to make long dangling lights to hang on our dead Christmas trees—but isn't Christmas supposed to be colourful? And our words are just forgotten, fading black and white photographs left in that old shoe-box by Grandma's old things.

To those close friends I lost to geography

Hands like Folded Paper

Don't press your hands into mine like folded paper, trusting my curiosity to spread the folds open and explore. Let your fingers mould into mine and let us become an attraction to those who want to see what true connection is. Like lost minds and wandering souls, we're just another two beings trying to make our way through this earth, falling into each other's laps by accident. We get certificates to show off our achievements to the world, but do they not realise that our art is a bigger achievement than any two-day event when others put words into our mouths? Fahrenheit 451, the degree where books catch fire, and think of all the literature and words and thoughts and mind stains considered immortalized that have gone up in smoke. Nothing about that is beautiful, nothing romantic, everything obscure. I don't pretend and my laughter is real, but you seem not to realise that that does not mean I am happy. Look me in the eye and ask, *Are you content?* and I think it would take all my strength not to burst into tears. Friends come and go, but there are some that should always stay and have a place in your heart, never mind your geographic location. People are always leaving, in one way or another, and each time a part of my heart is cut off. I want to gather you in my arms and just cry, because your departure means I lose a part of what has made me myself.

Miles are just another form of material and it can be overcome, connections can become deeper. But it also means that you're there and I'm here;

Abandoned. Alone.

Shell, Echo, Shadow, Machine

We're just shells of who we were
once, when we used to smile
and the world would light up,
innocent, happy, and naïve.

Our laughter is just an echo
of what it used to sound like
everyday; it used to make others
smile and laugh with us in joy.

The smiles painted on our faces
are just a shadow of their old
magnificence, when we kept
our promises and people proud.

Our heartbeats are just mechanical;
we forget we're meant to exist.

Just This Moment

A shimmer in the corner of a half-closed eye
deceives and perceives a wave of anguish,
falling, rolling, splashing on the shore.
Pushing back the golden yellow sand
because nothing is that pure,
that small and fine. Digging into beauty
and throwing it back up in the air,
messing around with it,
changing it into something it's not.

Lips crash violently against the tide
and try to hide the passion and anger
that birthed their power.
Just grip, hold on, and perhaps
you'll stay and not end up
in some random world,
where everyone talks, walks,
and even strays the same.

Lose yourself in pointless beauty
and pinpoint the time that your life
took its turn for the better,
and forget every twist it took
that left you lost, cold, and hungry.

Catch and stroke a butterfly,
in another lifetime or this one.
Paint all the colours
that you see in the sky

to create the world's one masterpiece,
then hide it amongst the clouds.

Live, breathe, and forget how
to curse, for a mere moment.

Ripped from Harmony

Dust accumulates on books decades old
and I try to shift my reality into a tiny vinyl
so that it can be seen, touched, and smelt,
and perhaps, someday, when analysed
thoroughly, understood. Wide open lips do me
no good and everyone can lie behind
their teeth, so don't say a word. I'll tell myself
what I want to hear. Then, I can say
you never lied.

A feathery touch tickles and soothes
the remains of a horrific burn;
gentle licks scrape soft, scarred skin,
its tissue twice as hard go through. Try
to cut through my pain and I'll make
my ache yours, and you'll stay in this
mental institution that is my mind forever.

For I cannot let any who love me leave,
for who, then, would come back?

Wrapped in Band-Aids

I was thinking earlier today about newspapers and faded lettering, young love and rock, paper, scissors. I tried to remember why I love injecting metaphors into my words and why I love reading them, the river in my mind overflooding. We take each other's hands and swear oaths, but who knows what it is you swear in your mind, forever or just a day? So we trust our badly torn senses, wrapped up in band-aids waiting to be ripped off. And when you sound that expected "ow" and rub the sore skin underneath, do you ever stop to wonder what would've happened if you'd kept the wound away from view? Just let it heal, hidden? Scars are just a permanent etch of life and you knew that, though maybe you never realised it. When you knit your hands with mine, will you make sure you cover all the gaps? For if there's a gap, there's a way for us to come undone.

Effervescent (Only on Holiday)

Perils of a life I don't want to recall, ties to a land and people I no longer want to know. The land I loved is far and I miss little. And how I want to keep it that way. Its populace was (and is) my defence. But right now I want out of my life, to take a longer break. I want a light at the end of the tunnel, something to spark and lead me . . . like how fireflies light up the river, lights on a Christmas tree. And I wonder if that's where the idea for fairy lights came from. The gorgeous flicker of fireflies— living, breathing, being—pinpricks of light down a dirty, winding river. I forget the last time the world was that in tune with itself. The wind between our teeth as we whistle and laugh, gazing at stars that twinkle, just as fireflies twinkle and wink at me, around me, surrounding me in a circle of light, feigning warmth and love. And these new friends, holding onto my arms, my neck, my heart, make me feel like I'm worth something again, like I'm no longer a nobody. I'm worth so much, I'm rich in life. I want to enjoy foreign countries. Enjoy the beauty, not just go around shopping like I do back home. I refuse to be just another Barbie doll, undressing layer by layer as she looks for her Ken, forgetting her principles and herself. And I forgot myself once, but I'm trying to remember and I hope I can find someone to help me do so. They call me a book sometimes, but if I am, then I'm one with the corners folded. People remember old parts of me and flip back, but seem to ignore the present, the page the book is open to. How I hate folding pages, the crease that appears. And how the book is ruined. I am ruined. They continue to fold me and I can't stop them, but never stop trying.

Faded Faces and Old Melodies

Your eyes wander and you relive forgotten tapes with names stuck onto them, melodies of a friendship that no longer exists. Open purses with gaping mouths hiding manuscripts of lies in a place where only paranoids and thieves think to look. Pills spilled over a desk, gleaming pink, that you no longer take but never think to remove. Frames surround you, images of good times and sincere friendships, of winning awards and a near-perfect family—images of things you no longer have, slipping away from you, a gossamer in the shadows of your mind. Dig out the home videos and studio portraits and search the images for feeling. Old yearbooks open at pages of faded faces, names printed underneath for the day you want to remember. So play the old tape you found underneath your bed, listen to the rhythm that was once your life, and promise the world that you'll start living again.

We all want to forget but want to be the one who's remembered.

Memories Dissolve

I.

Childhood Girls

I forget names of childhood friends who once
smiled with me and held my hand, asking me
if I knew how to play rope with their chants
and teaching me new ones, girls of my own age
but who seem so different than I, with a head
of braids in their hair for an early sophistication
that I did not possess, my own hair swinging
from its ponytail, tightly wrapped and safe.

II.

Simpler, Cleaner, More Articulate

I think I suffer memory loss deliberately because
sometimes when I think back I can hardly remember
if I was even alive, but I am told that I was.
So things slip from my mind and are blown away
like dandelion seeds into the wind where everyone
else can remember my thoughts and memories,
just not me. I am trapped in the present.

I grip onto a chimera of happiness but I know
that despite the materialistic things in my life,

I am not. Love is something I wish would bloom
inside of me again like a phoenix being reborn
from the ashes in my stomach, the blackest
of ashes (those of indifference), and fill me up
so much inside till I explode or have to somehow
eject this phoenix of love.

Memories dissolve consciously; I remember things
and suffer for it, and so decide that forgetting
would be so much simpler, cleaner, more articulate.

III.

Faded Petal

His face used to be sharp, clear-cut as glass,
and I would cut my fingertips on the edges
continuously as I surveyed with pride that
which I loved, smiling with the knowledge
that he was simply beautiful and uncouth.

He became a silhouette, a lovely outline
of what it is I would always want in a boy,
a gangly figure who would wrap his spidery
fingers around my wrist for no reason and
smile; I knew that something like this boy's silhouette
is all I would ever ask for, long arms for safety.

He is transformed again, he's soft light, fading
at dusk. Direct light no longer bathes him in glory,

the sun has laid its last kiss upon him and now,
softly stroking him, it begins its farewell, shining
faintly around his hair, making no secret of its fond
goodbye, taking away that sweet glint in chocolate eyes.

He's faded now, like old rose petals left outside
too long. His lips are no longer beautifully pink
but a tinted white; he's what we have to learn
to throw out, that which we are attached to
and no longer have in full, we learn how to let go.

I try to remember the face of this boy I used to love
but he's as fragile as new shoots and as dangerous as shattered glass.
My memory dissolves his chocolate eyes and flushed face,
untangles his golden hair from between my fingers and says,

you are not allowed to remember.

Wedding

Flashes go off several times a minute,
freezing this day, these lustrous moments,
for that satin-bound book of memories.

Like a butterfly she amazed, majestic,
and beautiful, *so very beautiful,*
in her high chair, glittering
with jewels, diamonds and rubies
that couldn't outshine her.

She sat, drowning in a sea
of turquoise fabric, lined with silver
and gold, swaying around her,
hugging her hips, a frame
boasting a gorgeous picture
of a young woman.

Sparks of Pain

Searing pain brings me to my senses, sparking from my forearm and extending like a spider's web to eternity. The flesh feels bruised, broken. It should be black and blue and yellow, colours mixing and clashing like a palette or a kaleidoscope, but it's the same pale pink it always has been. The bruised flesh remains an empty canvas, yet to be painted on with mischievous lips. Prodding the bicep only produces a violent twitch, and I proceed to gently press melodies into my flesh as ineptly as I would play a piano. I rub it softly, amazed at the feeling produced from this monotonous ache, as if death gripped it for a while, then thought the better of its actions and let it go. The tendons stretch and relax ceaselessly, wearing the elastic to a thin strip of forgotten plastic. I wonder what awkward position the night had been spent in, with my arm twisted or folded and tucked under my head like a pearl in an oyster. The pain fades as I stop extending my arm to reach for books and smiles and I cease to try and touch apparent beauty, like reality can satisfy me. I realise that, as with all pain, it only appears when we try to reach for things better left alone; dreams painted in skies and a flash of teeth with final goodbyes.

For Anne Behan

A Unique Being

I am known for being verbose in nature but if I really want
to find out my mind I write a poem and see what it is I think.
And so I find myself at a keyboard, thinking, waiting for
the inspiration to come to my fingers and paint an image
of what it is crossing my mind. So delicate yet not in the least
bit fleeting, this impression will stay upon my mind's paper
like a child walking with a dripping paintbrush, leaving stains
behind. This influence will leave a beautiful impromptu scar.

Except there are no words for what you mean to me, although
I wish so deeply I could pluck them out of the air and breathe
life into the letters of the alphabet. I fail and wonder if I've lost
my talent or if I've found someone too unique to be immortalized
in words. But know that if I could say anything I would thank
you repeatedly until you exclaim that I sound like a parrot
you'd like to strangle, or a scratched record in a forgotten player.

But thankful I am, and I feel so lucky to have been able to have
you in my life for the past few years, especially the two that have
just passed us by—and I don't know if it was easy to put up with me,
but you did it wonderfully and oftentimes sarcastically to the point
where I would smile and realise, *this is the point where
I should've stopped.* And I think there's only every so often
that someone is lucky and blessed enough to have a teacher
so wonderful and talented who pushes them forward and who somehow,
somewhere along the line, became trusted and a friend.

For Dana Khalaf

My Forever Friend

You're that person that I would run to when
I'm in need or just want, and I would tell
you all that had crossed my mind and we'd
talk it through and figure out a way to solve
it or maybe just half the pain by sharing it.

And you know, you're the one I love most,
the longest friend I've known and I know
that you'll always be there for me, no matter
what happens, because our friendship is like
no other, we can't describe it in words.

I've tried to write us many a poem but
I rarely find the words to weave together
of how much you mean to me; and who else
do I have a sixth sense with? Because we feel
each other's pain and neither of us can explain
it but when we're in extreme need of someone
(of each other), we can sense it and there's
no one I would rather share that with than you.

You're the person that first comes to mind
when I think, *who will I know forever*?
And I smile when I realise it'll always be true.
You're more than a best friend: you're a sister
and we share our hearts with each other for
you'd protect mine from harm as if it were yours.

Your sugar rises and you're afraid, but I'll be
there always and hold your hand throughout
whatever ordeal you have to face, because
we're indestructible, we make a perfect team.

You're the force that likes to remind me:
it does take more muscles to frown than to smile.

IV.

Live and Breathe Art

That which is Art about Art

Scream Art

We dissolve and corrode in our own memories
of faults and scraped knees, of little children
who bullied us and now, looking back, seem
so breakable and fragile; how were we ever scared?

We hide tokens behind in our childhood just in case
we get a ticket back someday so that we can look
into a string of evil eyes and see our lives floating by,
not quickly and in one breath but slowly, like our brains
are on backward speed, our relative velocity is
negative in relation to that of the rest of time.

We wonder when we will stop painting
lipstick mouths and girls with smooth, glossy legs;
when will we be true to ourselves and appear
natural, our legs unshaven, and refuse to conform?
So we paint what we cannot yet be, perhaps
never can become, and let the world beg of us
to decipher our unconventional paintings:
we are only worthy when we decide to cross boundaries.

We used to love being trapped in candy-striped
hula-hoops, flinging our hips and counting past
a hundred, laughing as we break our best friend's
records, being admired, applauded, and receiving
powdery kisses on our foreheads from our mothers
saying, "congratulations, sweetheart" and asking
if we would show them how good we are. Never mind
that we were not always good, never mind that we hurt

people sometimes in an effort to be called wonderful.

We are those girls who refused to wear shorts
underneath their dresses to go to school, but ran
anyway, our underwear flashing until our mothers
realised and forced us to choose between being a lady
and wearing shorts underneath our dresses, to hide
the shame of being told what colour underwear we had on.

We are the girls who loved art, but even at eight years
had formed our own opinions, breezily claiming Van Gogh's
flowers stupid, Picasso a genius. When we saw the Mona Lisa
we snorted, asking what was so important about her mundane
smile and disregarding Da Vinci's artwork, shaking our heads
(as if we were adults) and walking out of the Louvre, saying,
That was pathetic, not nearly worth its surrounding hysteria.

We've grown now, we're the in-betweens, the girls who
nobody knows quite what to do with, not old enough
to be taken too seriously but too old to be ignored.

We're the ones with avid opinions of our own and dark
eyeliner in sharp lines around our eyes, kohl weaved carefully,
reading whenever possible and constantly creating: poetry,
paintings, photography. We visit the galleries that no one
else knows what to make of, befriend new authors and artists,
swapping ideas, relating our work to each other's.

We go to artists' houses and spend hours pouring over
their work with them, feeling colour and texture and getting
re-inspired, realising our dreams between two lines of colour

scratched into a surface of acrylic and mixed media. We learn
from those artists and create our own work, shrouded in
our identity, work that may seem simple or otherwise
too complicated; yet we are more conceptual than you,
we dare to have our work free, elastic, to be understood
on many different levels that we ourselves did not consciously mean.

Our art does not always define us (we are too much for that),
but our work will continually define those who relate to it.

Irony, Loveless, Heart

If I were a painting, I'd be of limited colour
and blurred contours; work thick with texture
and mystery. The painting would be black
with smudged grey outlines and razor-sharp
streaks of white added as an afterthought.

And someone would be trying to force colour
in, thin but vivid lines of red and yellow,
to highlight the shadows and skeletons
in the background and make them look attractive.
The yellow would be worked over, only minute
glimpses through the thick grey and black
would be seen; the red left as it was, forced.

The painting would be done with precision
but it would be abstract and surreal, conceptual
work instead of clear and defined; a million
shades of grey. Words would be strewn in
the background: (i)rony, (love)less, he(art).

If I were a painting, I'd be one studied but
never quite understood, and it would be years
before someone noticed the violet streak
in the backdrop, worked over with black.

Create

Structures hanging in air;
fragile, elegant outlines
beautifying our silhouettes,
smudges of flaking charcoal
turned into straight, sharp
edges, into reality from
the storm of fiction's words
and paintings, wonderfully
crafted with mud rock drying,
its aroma the anthem of those
among us: ingenious or
misunderstood, simply creating.

Not My Words

These words that are so important
to us are just shells of what they mean.
We riddle our stanzas and paragraphs
with parentheses and metaphors, explaining
how a heart could beat itself to death,
and we fill them with juxtaposition
to try to forget that there's grey
in between, where the black and white
have mixed in swirls, a tornado tearing
through our lives and leaving behind
a mess of words, which we have to
pick up and throw away or rearrange
artistically.

These are my words, but they're not
because they're the same words you use,
just not in the same order. The only
difference is I remember to forget
half the pain when I write, because
writing in agony in something unpredictable,
you never know where you may end up,
or how your pain will shape the words
on your page. Just remember not to
fold the corners and move on to another
chapter, filled with the life you know
you deserve.

Write Me a Metaphor

These words are just pressed thoughts
upon a page, fragile like crumbling leaves,
golden on the ground and vulnerable;
stepped on so easily and disregarded,
beauty so frequently ignored.

We just write what we don't want
to even hope to believe is true.
We are the ones responsible for
longings of 'happily ever after'
and love at first sight; and we
apologise, because we just want
someone to go through the same.

We throw metaphors and similes
into the world in hundreds, about
everything that parades through
our lives, and we wonder when
someone will write us metaphors
and similes, likening us to willow
trees and flowing waters, claiming
we are beautiful.

We write like we breathe and that
is why our words often feel like
someone squeezing your throat,
choking you into oblivion, because
we write like we breathe.

We write life.

A Quill's Touch

You are like the quill that rests between
my fingers, something old and outgrown
that you dig up to feel superior or
inferior, to remember your place and not
forget that you draw your own destiny
on pages stained with your toil
throughout the years. You make me
remember that I am as insignificant
as the quill that rests in my hand,
forgotten and rarely glimpsed—but
the quill offers hope for some, showing
them the talent they always had.

Nibs Press Patterns

I feel the nib of my quill scratch the surface
of the sheet I am writing on and I smile, feeling
a connection with the writers of old who used to
sit by their windows to salvage the last
of the sun's soft beams before turning
away to light their candles and squint their eyes
to try to finish what they had started:
their masterpiece.

I feel the nib press patterns into the sheet
and I smile as I stain it with my thoughts,
thinking of proud old ladies with snow-white
hair and crow's-feet at the edges of their eyes
and mouths, wrinkles that I admire and regard
as immense beauty, proof of a life well lived.
I feel their presence and advice floating
around me as I inhale their sweet musk and
talcum powder scent; I understand their warnings.

I feel the nib dig into the sheet laid out so pure,
and I regard the elegant quill with which I script,
and realise I am not those writers of old.

I am a passing echo of their memory.

Soulless Artist

So you think you're an artist; just because
your body begs for food other than caffeine
and you write poetry on coloured pieces of paper
in fancy lettering, you think you're art itself
as you cower in a corner beside the River
Thames, under the red bridge across the street
from where Shakespeare's Globe stands proud.

Yes, you are an artist, but for different reasons
than you may think. You're an artist in your
imperfections as you scribble yet another poem
or verse and let it float down to the water to be
cleansed; you loose your soul a little more
every time you throw away something you wrote.

And in that way, my dear, you are an artist,
for most artists are missing a part of their soul.

Action Art of Life

You walked across my heart,
leaving imprints in black and blue,
bruising the very core
of my existence with care,
taking away all fuel and need
and replacing it with a kiss
of life, reviving me, letting
me be reborn into a world
of colour and needless beauty,
of film and roll, of lens focusing
and shutters clicking, paint
dripped and splattered. Action
art of life, the irrationality
of loving and being in danger
from yourself.

Speculate

You're so
in love
with

September's dances
and December's kisses;

you dance
so prettily

with autumn
leaves.

You play
with words

like
they're property,

and wonder
of stars

like our planet
is not enough.

Artist

My head is spinning like the propellers of the plane
I'm in, shooting through the air with me,
challenging the rules of life, how humans should stay
on their own two legs, touching the soil, touching
ground, feeling the dirt beneath their feet and underneath
their toenails, like the earth's blood seeping
into the creases between our sunken palms,
hugging our warmth and bleeding into us, because
we're all a part of the earth, as the earth is a part of us.

I'm being driven insane by the thumping in my head
but insane is relative, and who knows what it is
really that takes away our reasoning? My tears spill
into your hands and you try to grasp them tightly
but they slip from between your fingers, between
the clefts in the stone like the Grand Canyon, orange
and enormous, from working with clay
and your beautiful artwork, amazing pieces
that make me gaze into the hairline fissures
lovingly because I couldn't possibly recreate works
such as these. You're a fantastic artist with your
greasy hair and wide mouth, biting off your own lips
as you concentrate, throwing material around,
and you constantly amaze me and I wish I could amaze one day.

Your art pieces hung in air feel like they defy gravity,
just as you defy petty human affairs and interactions.

V.

Thoughts Revealed

Matters of the World

You Paint War

You paint destruction on the inside of our eyelids
so we can't ever close our eyes and forget what
it is you're doing to the world, destroying homes
and tearing apart families, killing brothers and
mothers, disregarding lost fathers and sisters;
you paint them in the backdrop in camouflage,
make us try to believe they are not important.

But you forget there are some who can look
past the propaganda that is the eight o'clock news
and your face and stuttering voice, realising
we are being slowly destroyed. Your country rises
against the killing of your men, but the killing
of our men is accepted—you rocked the country
to the brink of civil war.

You paint disasters into life, you've got a way to
disrupt the world and can always murmur veto
with a smug smile when you don't agree, stop
the world from advancing and kill all organized
religion, thought, belief.

But you forget that someday we will gain
enough power to stop you and put someone
in your place that deserves your position.
You forget, you represent millions of people
who don't share your warped ideas, who take
to the streets and demonstrate for peace,
shouting in sync, "No more blood for oil."

Crimson Death

Shock. Horror.

A fresh wave of grief.
One shot. Two shots.
Two people. *Dead.*

Blood.

Bodies left for the shadows
to indulge.

Death:
metallic,
bitter.

Anger and frustration.
Those soldiers had no right.

I cried a river of blood;
in this goblet, a few drops,
crimson.

Mr. President:
Drink.

He Ambles

Limbs twisted into grotesque shapes
wrapped around a short, thin stump;
bodies distorted, positions unnatural.
A man, ambling along—with a gun.

Lives, so precious, are rendered cheap;
with one pull another is ended.
So the wives, children, and mothers
sit at home hoping for any miracle.

His hands are filthy,
drenched and stained with blood;
the Nile's waters would not be enough
to cleanse this murderer of sticky crimson.

He ambles down a well-worn path,
a bullet for everyone strapped to a pole;
brains blown out; body doesn't fall,
for it's already on the ground.

Vietnam War

"Hey! Hey! LBJ! How many kids did you kill today?"
– Popular anti-war chant during the Vietnam War

So we read about wars like they're just a mess of blood and limbs
at imperative timings when the world is wishing for peace all around
and we forget that these wars are people's choices, from the country
who declares it to the soldiers that fight against it, and we all don't like
war, we all know what war brings, but do we really? Do people really
pay attention to things that happen, that they see on their TV screens?
Or is it like clips from a movie, something you disregard because
they say *don't trust television*; so you trust what you want to and forget
what you don't want to remember. But what do you do when you can't,
like that little girl running naked up a hill because the Americans
dumped napalm on her village and she's burning alive, and for how long?
Those wounds won't even begin to heal for six months, that's if
she lives through the pain and it doesn't burn through her muscle
and bone; and if they know how horrible it is, why do it? The President
says that it's for freedom and they're fighting for it, but your soldiers
have peace signs painted on their helmets like a tattoo, because it's not
going to fade away, it's a decision based on fact and horror, not a whim.

And what does it tell you when a monk would rather burn himself, set
himself on fire and burn alive, than live in a country you're claiming
to free from oppression? Tell me, Presidents, how you sleep at night
knowing that you've killed your country's spirit and tens of thousands
of your own men in a war that cannot be won, a war that should not
have even been fought. So Ho Chi Minh is a communist and he will kill
those who stand in his way but you've just added a million and over
to the toll. I'm not saying I'm for the communists but if you're going

to try and free a country, you should not terrorize its people and expect them to support and love you. And don't be shocked when a six-year-old on a bicycle throws a hand grenade into your nightclubs as you lose your wits and get drunk; why are you so surprised, when you frag your officers to avoid your duties? Killing for so long and so much is wrong and it'll silence your heart because how can you possibly retain feelings and do what you have to? Like the soldiers at My Lai, slaughtering an entire village, four hundred people in five hours because they thought they were Vietcong. But as it turned out, those were innocent civilians caught in the cross fire, and some civilians have to die in a war but four hundred in five hours is a number I can't wrap my head around like a stick figure, it's too much for sixty men to kill four hundred unfeelingly. They were told that these were the enemy and to execute them, so they did, down to the last old man, woman, and child. This war is a war that cannot be won; it's a war against the dominoes, but how do you even know that the dominoes would have fallen if you hadn't intervened? Tell me, Eisenhower, Kennedy, Johnson, Nixon, Ford—which of you caused its downfall, which of you sealed its fate?

You rendered a beautiful country with riches to a scarred barren land and threw their traditions away like old rags ripped by a zealous dog, but they prevailed and you failed, they managed to get back onto their feet.

So tell me, how do you feel about the war now? What would you have changed?

Represent

Reality always waits. It springs on us when we are in our deepest well of fantasy. Mundane existence in third—no, *fourth*-world countries. How do they survive being harshly stripped of their lives? How do they thrive as they wade through puddles of blood and rivers of tears? In a country where only three colours exist; black and white photographs that somehow collect red, red blood. No gorgeous illusions here. Love's young dream doesn't exist. Innocence is not a word. Here, you are born wary and grow wise. You learn which blocks to avoid and how to hear the deadly hum of machinery; you learn to leave your family lying on the ground as you run and hide. You learn to kiss your spouse's dead lips goodbye and how to pile rubble onto a corpse that was once your best friend. **Represent necessity** and watch as the clouds part and trails of already-forgotten smoke fill the sky. Watch as they play "tag, you're it" in the sky. Drop. Roll. You define camouflage. Drop. Roll. Stay still.

Throw your hands up towards the sky and stand. **Represent time.** You died inside long ago and you've become so in tune. You know, *you just know.* So when the first drop of rain in a year falls, you catch it because you were there first. Watching. Waiting. You have a fallen angel guiding you. Listen to the slow throb of your heart. Gather all the air and scream loudly. Make yourself a target.

Let these endless bombs try to steal the wisdom in your eyes. Let this spray make you collapse on the ground. Kiss the asphalt and laugh loudly at those who try to kill you and, in doing so, grant you immortality. Raise your hands up and dip your fingers in the sky. Taste the tips and see whether you can detect God's salty tears. Grab a cloud tightly and tug it down. Pull it down, down, down. Wear it, and become one with the world. **Represent life.**

VI.

Stained Paper

Etched Forever

Beautiful Characters

I.

Dearest Beatrice, how I love your witty repartee
as I see your (soon-to-be) lover struggle
to come up with a retort more pronounced and exaggerated.
Oh! how you claim that you would rather hear your dog
bark at crow than a man swear he loves you—but
when love arrives you greet it with sarcasm veiling devotion.
My dear, how lucky Signor Mountanto is to have landed
such sure love, fit for mountains and lullabies.

Darling Benedick, how I adore your monologues
and how sure you are that you truly love none
while your (soon-to-be) lover stands parallel
to you. And oh! how quickly you challenge
your friend to a duel when she begs it of you.
(Like the speed at which you fell into the trap they set.)

Baby Catrin, with your red rope of love, trailing
love and conflict upon those you hold dear.
How you show us that love is inseparable from incongruity,
as our ties with the woman whose womb we were in
is a constant two-way tension. Oh! to have been taught
the lesson by other than Mistress Experience.

Poor Jane, with your governess' dress and firm mouth,
unaware of the terrible attic secret, ignoring cries
as we so often like to do. How Mr. Rochester wronged you,
but he paid for it with his sight and oh! how happy you are

now, with his and your first-born as you stand before him
in your pale blue dress and glittering ornament, and he
remarks on the child's inheritance of his large black eyes.

Bloody Macbeth, how you let things go. Thane of Glamis
was not enough, nor was Thane of Cawdor. All hail, Macbeth!
Hail to thee—who shall be pronounced an eradicator.
Oh! how sin speaks to one with incessant currents of gold,
promising the improbable and making the impossible
happen. But the spirit of Banquo will continue to rise
and, dear murderer, Macduff shall not fail. As promised,
Great Birnam Wood to High Dunsinane Hill shall come.

Sad Edward, how your hands cut clean (quick and painful
and not meant). How poignant you are with your chalk-white
face as your tears form long stalactites down your cheek.
You hurt the ones you love the most, and oh! how like
Frankenstein you are—made on a steel table, an experiment.
But Scissorhands, you were deliberate, not a mistake,
like so many of us who call ourselves real are.

Imperfect characters, how I love you all,
you show me so brilliantly that none of us is complete.
You show us how sometimes we must live
through the fire to find love, be sliced to understand,
fight for ourselves against those we love, change
our minds when we discover we have been wrong,
and not believe everything we are told.

II.

Patient Clare, your very hair is a juxtaposition
to your personality, flaming red against the calm
blue of your soul, making your way through
life with several miscarriages, losing one baby
after another, toils that leave behind little signs
on your weary body, scars and stretch marks
that Henry has grown to love, like he loves you,
unconditionally. Oh how drained you are
as you wait for your lover to come home
from another time, yet most probably still with you.

Beautiful Dorian, with your hidden canvas rotting
in the playroom upstairs as it breathes in
the atmosphere and turns childish games
into images of sin (catch me if you can), lying
and trying to deceive the world with your beauty,
petals for lips and gold hair, hoping to never
be marred, your canvas wrinkled and dimpled
in all the wrong places and silver takes over
the golden halo placed wrongly upon your head.
Oh, Dorian, with your soul stolen or borrowed,
your ever sweet nature destroyed—the devil blew
into you, for you now feel nothing as you see death.

Dearest Polly, with your nimble hands
and countless sacrifices, you present yourself
so serenely to the world in black silk
as they mock you needlessly for your poverty.
My little blackbird, you are more beautiful
than they and your strength and peace of mind

is what dear Tom will fall for; you will find
your partner in him and you will be happy.

Darling Sara, how hard they made you work,
scrubbing at floors and being looked down
upon, a princess brought to her knees
by some twists of fate; but oh, my dear,
you will be discovered and your fortune
returned to you, and even in the hands
of comfort you remember the misfortunate
and dole out buns at your expense.
Such a sweet nature you have; you will
make an amazing lady and any man
would be lucky to have you by his side.

Eccentric BFG, you knew that every human
bean is diddly and different, that some of us
are scrumdiddlyumptious and some uckyslush.
I am one of those who gobblefunk around
with words, friendly giant, but I think that you do,
too, but don't realise it. I think all of us
who got to know you need to thank you because
you introduced dreams of catching dreams
in our young minds and made us smile.

Imperfect characters, how I love you all;
you show me so brilliantly that none of us are complete.
You show us how sometimes we must love
unconditionally, prepare to age gracefully,
learn how to sacrifice, believe that we are important,
and understand that we're all unique.

Beautiful characters, how I love to surround myself with you.

Fickle and Imaginative

You're in love with the improbable
and believe in the impossible
but don't appreciate satire
and have forgotten beauty.

You pierce your own ears
and you numb yourself
with ice but your heart beats
twice as fast as your eyes spy
two red pearls on your pillow.

You think you can waltz
in and out of your own life
but you can't, no matter how
beautiful the dance, because
your mind is fickle but too
imaginative and what a lethal
combination you make.

Melt to Reveal

Tell me, will you still be there when the frost melts
and the red rose shows you its true brilliance?
Will you remain unconditionally by its side, when
the rose hugs its own thorns to protect its core
from the icy world, desperate not to be snipped,
cut down. Dying only to garnish another's home,
to warm someone's heart; beautiful crimson
corpse, dangerous yet serene—seeing, feeling,
flashing red before my broken eyes (are you there?),
melting to blend into the frost, abstract streaks
of white and red, mixed and shaken together.

This World

Blood is seen pour out
and the pain is comprehended,
the ache is all around,
dead bodies swim in filth.

The tears are known to fall,
but when felt
there is no trace,
body has become
too efficient to disgrace.

A sigh escapes lips,
marred by expression on face,
rouge painted on
hides sorrow kept far off.

Freedom is a prisoner
that all seek to find,
but people don't expect
to look for it in skies.

The sun shines brightly,
burning holes in little hearts,
eyes glitter menacingly;
this world is no more than art.

Sijo Poems

*Sijo is a Korean poem consisting of 44 to 46 syllables in three lines,
with 14 to 16 syllables each line. Sometimes it is written in six lines,
the three lines split in two. It has a beginning in Line 1, development
in Line 2, and conclusion with a twist or surprise ending in Line 3.*

I Start

A breathless, dark and gloomy night,
      raindrops, and hardly any other sounds.

I start and shiver at a noise
      and step into the flowerbed.

As I look around I see
      a pair of glowing yellow eyes.

Shiver

I shiver at the silky touch,
      this cool caress which sooths me so.

I arch myself back in content
      and run my hand down past my thigh.

A smile tugs at my cold lips;
      I turn up the air conditioning.

Plagiarizer

You think you can steal
our flames from our candles
without asking, that you can
take our brilliance, making it
your own, when we try so hard
to make our words shine.

Index of Titles

Laala Kashef Alghata is a sixteen-year-old poet and novelist. *Behind the Mask: A Folded Heart* is her second book. Her first, a children's novel called *Friendship in Knots*, was written while she was ten and eleven and published two years later. Writing, reading, and art are her main passions, and her greatest wish is to study at Cambridge or Oxford and continue her promising professional writing career. She currently lives in Bahrain and attends Sixth Form College.